BRAiN BENDERS iNTERMEDiATE

Challenging Puzzles and Games for Math and Language Arts

Credits:
Editor: Julie Kirsch
Layout Design: Chasity Rice
Cover Design: Chasity Rice
Cover Illustration: Bill Neville, Mike Duggins

Printed in the USA • All rights reserved.　　　　　ISBN 978-1-60022-312-9

TABLE OF CONTENTS

RB-904083 Brain Benders   © Rainbow Bridge Publishing

NUMBERS IN A LINE

Consecutive numbers are numbers that follow one after the other. Write the consecutive numbers that answer the questions below.

1. Which three consecutive numbers add up to 123? _40-41-42_

2. Which three consecutive odd numbers add up to 123? _39-41-43_

3. Which three consecutive numbers add up to 456? _151-152-153_

4. Which three consecutive even numbers add up to 456? _150-152-154_

5. Which three consecutive numbers add up to 789? _292-293-294_

6. Which three consecutive even numbers add up to 150? _48-50-52_

7. Which four consecutive odd numbers add up to 240? _57-59-61-63_

8. Which five consecutive numbers add up to 100? _18-19-20-21-22_

9. Which five consecutive numbers add up to 150? _28-29-30-31-32_

10. Which five consecutive numbers add up to 500? _98-99-100-101-102_

RB-904083 Brain Benders

MISSING SIGNS

Add one operation sign (+, –, x, or ÷) and one equal sign (=) to each row to make an equation that is true. Write the equations on the lines.

Example: 9 3 3 3 9 3 0 ———————→ 933 – 3 = 930

1.   4 8 1 2 6 0 $48 + 12 = 60$

2.   5 5 5 2 7 5   _____

3.   1 0 1 0 1 0 0 $10 \times 10 = 100$

4.   2 1 0 1 0 2 1   _____

5.   1 1 7 1 0 1 0 7 $117 - 10 = 107$

6.   6 3 5 7 6 2 8   _____

7.   3 0 3 3 0 3 3 3   _____

8.   3 5 6 0 2 1 0 0   _____

9.   9 4 8 2 4 7 4   _____

10.   8 7 5 2 4 5 2 4   _____

RB-904083 Brain Benders

BACKWARD NUMBERS

A math teacher wrote math problems on the board for her class to copy. The problems are shown below.

32	74	45	17	46	56
+ 56	+ 58	+ 98	+ 82	+ 75	+ 54
___	___	___	___	___	___

The teacher assigned the problems for homework. Whitney was in a hurry, and she copied all of the problems backward. Whitney's problems are shown in the box at the right.

The next day, the students checked their work. The teacher called out the answers for each problem, and Whitney found that she had gotten every problem right!

23	47	54
+ 65	+ 85	+ 89
___	___	___

71	64	65
+ 28	+ 57	+ 45
___	___	___

How did Whitney do it? First, write the answers to all of the problems above. Compare the sums in both sets of problems. Explain why you got the results you did. Do you think that all two-digit addition problems will give you the same results?

_____

_____

_____

_____

_____

RB-904083 Brain Benders

NUMBER SWITCH

Marvin put number cards together to make math problems. However, for each problem he accidentally put two cards in the wrong places. Switch the numbers around and rewrite the problems to correct them.

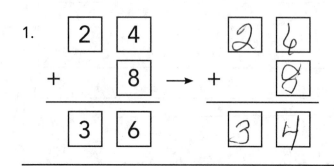

1.
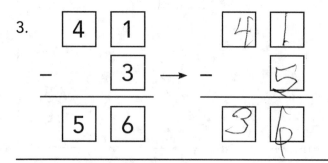

2.

3.

4.

5.

6.

7.

8.

RB-904083 Brain Benders

© Rainbow Bridge Publishing

CALCULATOR RIDDLES

Use a calculator to solve the problems below. Do not use the order of operations. Instead, do the calculations in the order they appear. Then, turn the calculator upside down to find the answer to each riddle. Write the answers on the lines.

1. 150 x 3 + 276 − 50 ÷ 2 = $450 + 276 = 726 - 50 = 676 - 338$

   Which animal is the best speller? A spelling ___Bee___

2. 18 ÷ 2 + 52 − 54 ÷ 0.5 = $9 + 61 = 70.5 \overline{)700}$ = 14

   What should you say when you meet a giant alien at your door? ___hi___

3. 2,001 x 20 ÷ 2 + 15,236 − 240 = _____

   What honks but isn't a car? _____

4. 96,900 − 60 ÷ 40 + 4,292 ÷ 0.5 x 4 = _____

   What things get larger the more you take away? ___holes___

5. 266,600 ÷ 31 − 445 ÷ 5 + 348 x 3 − 300 = _____

   What does a table have that you also have? ___Legs___

6. 363,636 ÷ 3 ÷ 36 + 33 x 17 − 4,755 = _____

   What comes in different sizes but are always one foot long? _____

7. 100 ÷ 0.0004 + 54,321 − 17 = _____

   What does the farmer say when he hears a good joke? _____

RB-904083 Brain Benders

A baker prepared several trays of cookies for sale. Then, the baker set out the trays and opened the door to the bakery.

Mrs. Lee was the first customer. She was buying cookies for her office luncheon. She looked at the trays and immediately bought ¼ of the cookies.

Next, Mr. Lang entered the bakery. He wanted to buy a treat for his students. Mr. Lang bought ½ of the cookies that were left on the trays.

Ms. Lopez was the third customer. She wanted to give her neighbor a birthday treat. She bought ⅓ of the remaining cookies.

Mrs. Brenner came next. She wanted to take cookies to her grandchildren. She bought ½ of the cookies that were left.

Mr. Murray was the fifth customer. There weren't many cookies left. He didn't want to seem greedy, so he bought only ⅓ of the cookies that were still on the trays.

Ryan walked into the bakery. He was hungry and wanted a quick snack. After he bought ½ of the cookies, only 4 cookies were left.

1. How many cookies did each customer buy?

Mrs. Lee _____24_____ cookies   Mr. Lang _____36_____ cookies

Ms. Lopez _____18_____ cookies   Mrs. Brenner _____12_____ cookies

Mr. Murray _____4_____ cookies   Ryan _____4_____ cookies

2. How many cookies did the baker set out for sale in the morning? _____96_____

RB-904083 Brain Benders

A FAMILY PORTRAIT

Mr. and Mrs. Jackson are having a family portrait taken with their son and daughter. The photographer wants to have two people sit in the front and two people stand in the back. The Jacksons have decided that they want to send a copy of their portrait to each of their relatives. However, they don't want any two portraits to be the same. Mr. Wilson has asked the photographer to place the family in as many different positions as possible.

How many different portraits are possible? Work out the solution in the space below.

Is there a quick way to find out how many arrangements are possible? For example, how many different arrangements would there be if there were 5 people in the family instead of 4?

_____

_____

_____

_____

_____

_____

RB-904083 Brain Benders

Solve the addition problems below to find an interesting number pattern.

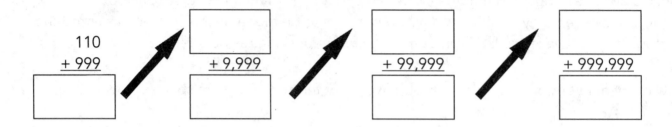

Continue the problems at least three more times.

What pattern do you see? _____

_____

_____

_____

_____

_____

_____

RB-904083 Brain Benders

MYSTERIOUS MULTIPLICATION

Multiply each of the following three-digit numbers by 11. Then, multiply each product by 91.

1. 413
   x 11
   413
   4,130
   4,543

2. 736
   x 11

3. 80
   x 11

4. 653
   x 11

5. 999
   x 11

4,543
x 91

x 91

x 91

x 91

x 91

Now, write three other three-digit numbers and multiply them in the same way.

Did you get the same results as above? Why do you think you got the answers that you did?

_____

_____

_____

_____

_____

_____

RB-904083 Brain Benders

The first three figures in each row were created from the same pattern. Study the pattern and fill in the missing number for the third figure. For the last figure in each row, use the pattern to make your own set of numbers.

1.

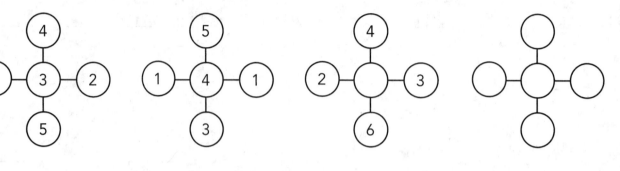

Describe the pattern. _____

_____

2.

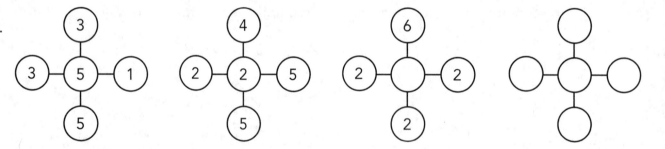

Describe the pattern. _____

_____

3.

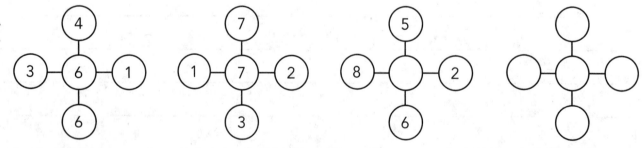

Describe the pattern. _____

_____

RB-904083 Brain Benders

DOTTED HEXAGONS

Hexagon A is made up of 6 dots.
Each side of the hexagon is made up of 2 dots.

Hexagon B is made up of 12 dots.
Each side of the hexagon is made up of 3 dots.

A. 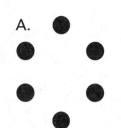 B.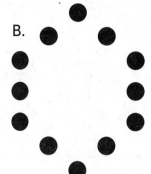

1. In the box, draw the next hexagon in the pattern.

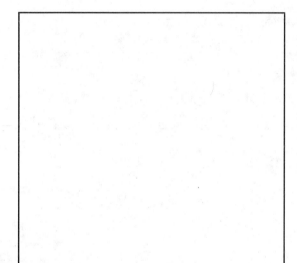

How many dots did you use? _____

How many dots are needed per side? _____

2. Complete the chart to show how many dots you would need to make dotted hexagons.

Dots per Side	2	13	4	5	6
Total Number of Dots	6	12			

3. Can you make a formula to help you figure out how many dots you will need for any dotted hexagon? For example, how many dots would you need for a hexagon that uses 20 dots per side? _____

_____

RB-904083 Brain Benders

PAPER PATTERNS

Ashley arranged paper squares to make a pattern:

1. If Ashley continues the pattern, how many squares will she use for the 10th figure?

   _____

2. How can you find the number of squares needed for any figure in Ashley's pattern?

   _____

   _____

Ryan used paper squares to make a different pattern:

3. If Ryan continues the pattern, how many squares will he use for the 10th figure?

   _____

4. How can you find the number of squares needed for any figure in Ryan's pattern?

   _____

   _____

RB-904083 Brain Benders

DOTS AND SQUARES

Look at the 3 x 3 arrangements of dots below. How many squares can be made from 9 dots if you use the dots to mark their corners? Use the grids below to show all of the squares that you can make. **HINT**: There are more than five squares.

Now, look at the 4 x 4 arrangements of dots below. How many squares can be made from 16 dots if you use the dots to mark their corners? Use the grids below to show all of the squares you can make. HINT: There are more than 13 squares.

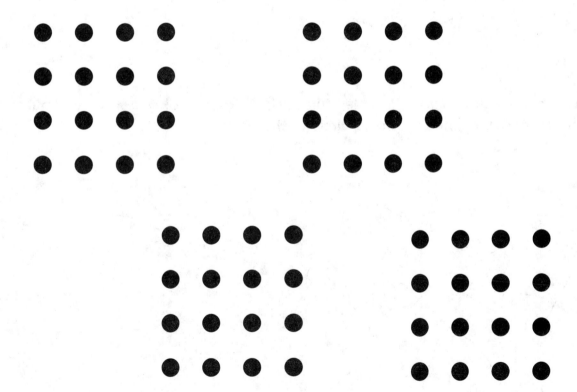

RB-904083 Brain Benders

CIRCLE PUZZLES

The pieces below are fourths of a circle. What will the circle look like when you put the pieces together? Draw the completed circle at the right.

The pieces below are fourths of a circle. What will the circle look like when you put the pieces together? Draw the completed circle at the right.

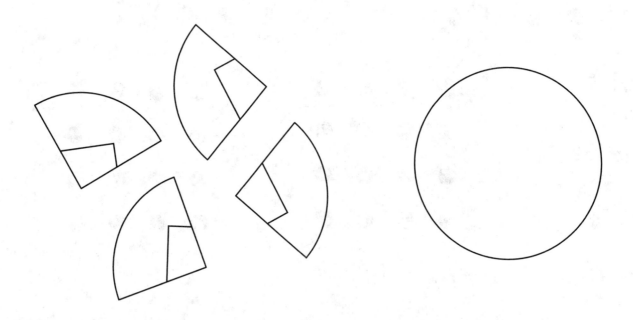

RB-904083 Brain Benders

Each shape in the grid stands for a number. The numbers around the grid are the sums you get when you add the numbers in a row or in a column. Write the number each shape stands for and fill in the three missing sums at the bottom of the grid.

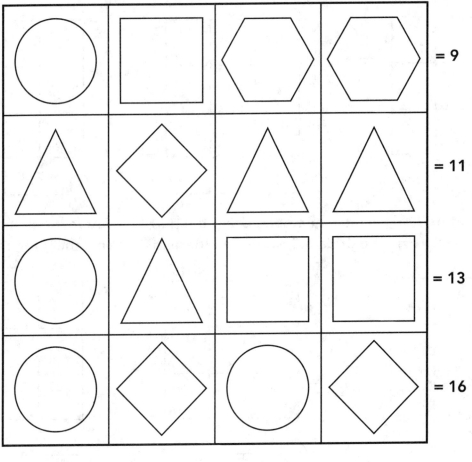

= 9

= 11

= 13

= 16

= 11   = ___   = ___   = ___

RB-904083 Brain Benders

NUMBER CUBES

Place the numbers 1–9 in the first grid so that the sums of the numbers in each row and column are the same number. Write the sum on the line after each row and under each column. Use graph paper to practice. Write your solution in the first grid. Then, solve the number cube again in two different ways.

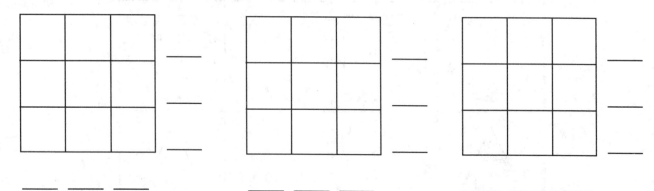

Take any set of 9 consecutive numbers. Using the patterns you found in the grids above, place the numbers in the grids below. Use a different set of numbers for each grid.

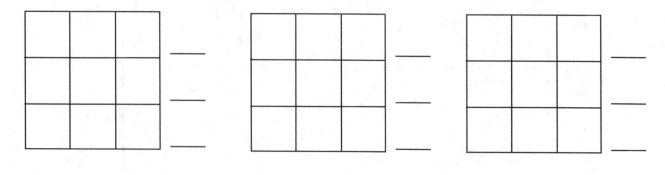

Fill in the grids below with multiples of 2, 3, and 4. Does the pattern still work? _____

multiples of 2   multiples of 3   multiples of 4

RB-904083 Brain Benders

NUMBER RIDDLES

Read carefully to solve each number riddle. Write your answer in the blank.

1. Divide me by 6 and add 3. Divide this by 3, then multiply by 4 to get 12.

   What number am I? _____

2. Multiply me by 3, then add 3. Divide this by 5, then subtract 4. The final answer is 2.

   What number am I? _____

3. Divide 24 by me, then multiply by 5. Subtract 7 and multiply by 7. You get 56.

   What number am I? _____

4. Divide me by 5. Subtract 9, then multiply by 6. Subtract 2, then multiply by 4 to get 16.

   What number am I? _____

5. Add 2 to me, multiply by 3, then subtract 9. Divide by 6, then add 4. You get 6.

   What number am I? _____

6. Divide 18 by me, then subtract 9. Add 1. Triple the answer. Add 6, then divide by 9. You get 4.

   What number am I? _____

7. Multiply me by 9, then subtract 104. Divide this by 5. Subtract 2, then divide by 8. Multiply this by 7. You get 21.

   What number am I? _____

8. Add 34 to me, then divide by 4. Multiply this by 5. Add 1 more. Multiply this by 2, then divide by 8. The final answer is 19.

   What number am I? _____

9. Divide me by 4, subtract 3, and then divide by 7. Multiply this by 8, then add 4. Divide by 4 to get 9.

   What number am I? _____

RB-904083 Brain Benders

FIND THE NUMBERS

Solve the equations in each set below. Each letter stands for a digit. Substitute each letter with a number to make the sets of equations true.

Set A

```
  M              T            M          M =
  M            x R          x M
  M              M           RM          R =
  M
+ T                                      T =
 TM
```

Set B

```
  B              J            B          B =
x B            + S          + B
 JS              B           SJ          J =

                                         S =
```

Set C

```
  G              G       Z + K + Z = G + G     G =
x G            – K
 ZK              K                             K =

                                               Z =
```

Set D

```
  U              C       G – U = C + C       G          C =
x G            x U                           G
 CG              U                           G          G =
                                             G
                                             G          U =
                                             G
                                           + G
                                            UG
```

RB-904083 Brain Benders

HiDDEN NUMBERS

Each puzzle below contains multiple ways to make a given answer. Any squares that touch can work together. Each number in the puzzle grid must be used at least once.

1. Using the numbers below, write 10 equations that equal 3.

8	2	2	2
4	1	6	9
10	7	2	5

$(8 \div 2 + 2) \div 2 = 3$ _____

_____ _____

_____ _____

_____ _____

_____ _____

2. Using the numbers below, write 10 equations that equal 5.

2	4	11	8
1	6	3	2
7	2	10	1

_____ _____

_____ _____

_____ _____

_____ _____

_____ _____

3. Using the numbers below, write 10 equations that equal 10.

6	2	3	1
2	7	5	4
1	8	3	9

_____ _____

_____ _____

_____ _____

_____ _____

_____ _____

RB-904083 Brain Benders

Add your way to the top. Add adjacent numbers and write the sum in the box above them. Use the numbers given to fill in the first row of steps.

A. 2, 4, 5, 6, 9

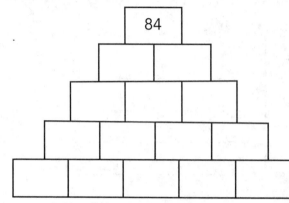

B. 1, 2, 3, 7, 8

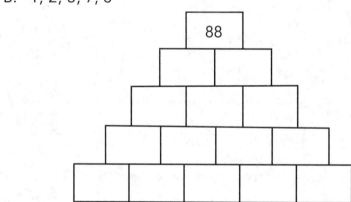

C. 2, 4, 6, 8, 9

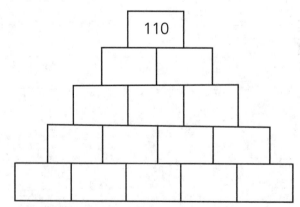

RB-904083 Brain Benders

MISSING STEPS

Add your way to the top. Add adjacent numbers and write the sum in the box above them. Use the numbers given to fill in the first row of steps.

A. 1, 3, 5, 6, 7

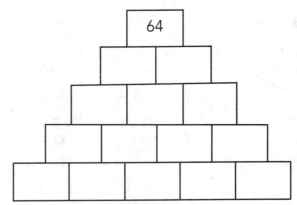

B. 2, 2, 3, 3, 4, 5

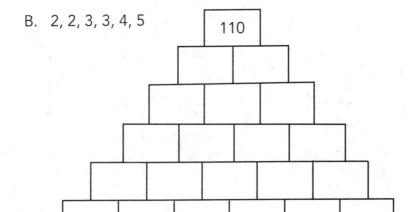

C. 1, 2, 5, 7, 8, 9

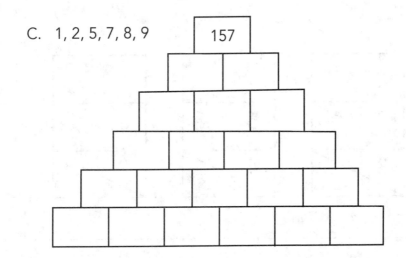

RB-904083 Brain Benders

PUZZLE IT OUT

Each set of puzzles uses the same rule to determine the answer in the top space of each box. Determine and explain the rule. Use the rule to fill in the remaining boxes.

Set A

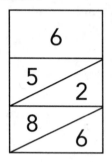 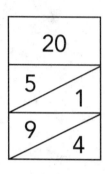 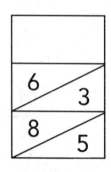 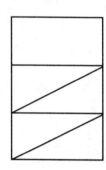

6	20	2		
5 / 2	5 / 1	9 / 7	6 / 3	
8 / 6	9 / 4	4 / 3	8 / 5	

Rule: _____

Set B

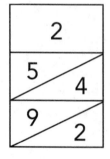 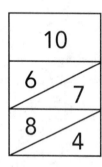 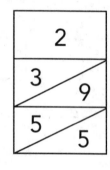 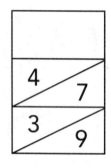 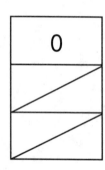

2	10	2		0
5 / 4	6 / 7	3 / 9	4 / 7	
9 / 2	8 / 4	5 / 5	3 / 9	

Rule: _____

Set C

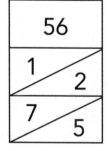 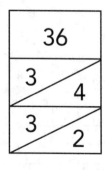 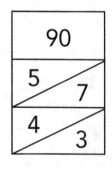 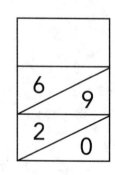

56	36	90		45
1 / 2	3 / 4	5 / 7	6 / 9	
7 / 5	3 / 2	4 / 3	2 / 0	

Rule: _____

RB-904083 Brain Benders

Use the clues below to find out where each person is hiding. Write each person's name in the spot where she is hiding. Read all of the clues before beginning.

	1	2	3	4	5
1					
2					
3					
4					
5					

1. Julie is not in any odd numbered rows or columns.
2. Paul said, "Look in column 2 to find me!"
3. Aidyn is in the row right after Paul.
4. Paul is in the next to the last row.
5. Aidyn is hiding in the same column as Julie.
6. No one else is hiding in Paul's row or column.
7. Henry is in the column before Julie and Aidyn.
8. Henry was found in the row between Julie and Paul.
9. Will is in row 3.
10. Will said, "Paul is hiding in the column just after me."
11. Alexis said, "No one else is in my row or column."

Melanie scored 5 different point totals in 5 different basketball games. Use the matrix and the clues below to determine the number of points Melanie scored against each team.

- When the team played the Bobcats, Melanie made only 3-point baskets.
- Melanie scored only 2-point baskets against the Hornets.
- Melanie scored fewer points against the Hornets than the Wolfpack.
- The points that Melanie scored against the Wolfpack were a multiple of 4.
- Melanie scored the most points against the Badgers.

	7	9	12	20	24
Badgers					
Bobcats					
Hornets					
Wolfpack					
Tornadoes					

Points against:

Badgers _____

Bobcats _____

Hornets _____

Wolfpack _____

Tornadoes _____

Use Melanie's point scores to find the scores of some of her teammates.

1. In the game against the Bobcats, Janet made as many 2-point shots as Melanie made 3-point shots. How many points did Janet score?_____

2. Add Melanie's scores against the Wolfpack and the Badgers. Divide this by the difference in her scores against the Bobcats and Wolfpack. This is the number of baskets Delia made in game 5. Half of her shots were worth 2 points, and the other half were worth 3 points. How many points did Delia score? _____

3. Sophie made as many baskets against the Hornets as Melanie did. Two thirds of her baskets were 2-pointers; the rest were 3-pointers. How many points did Sophie score?

MYSTERY SQUARES

1. Solve the mystery square below. Each column and each row must have a sum of 110.

   Numbers to Use: 32, 33, 34, 35, 36, 37, 38, 39, 40, 41, 42

   (Note: Each number can only be used once.)

			= 110
			= 110
			= 110
= 110	= 110	= 110	

2. Solve the mystery square below. Each column and each row must have a sum of 350.

   Numbers to Use: 112, 113, 114, 115, 116, 117, 118, 119, 120, 121, 122

   (Note: Each number can only be used once.)

			= 350
			= 350
			= 350
= 350	= 350	= 350	

RB-904083 Brain Benders

MYSTERY SQUARES

1. Solve the mystery square below. Each column and each row must have a product of 120.
   Numbers to Use: 1, 2, 3, 4, 5, 6, 7, 8, 9, 10, 11, 12, 13, 14, 15
   (Note: Each number can only be used once.)

			= 120
			= 120
			= 120
= 120	= 120	= 120	

2. Solve the mystery square another way.

			= 120
			= 120
			= 120
= 120	= 120	= 120	

RB-904083 Brain Benders

MYSTERY TRIANGLE

Complete the mystery triangle. Each side should have a sum of 350.

Numbers to Use: 112, 113, 114, 115, 116, 117, 118, 119, 120, 121, 122

(Note: Each number can only be used once.)

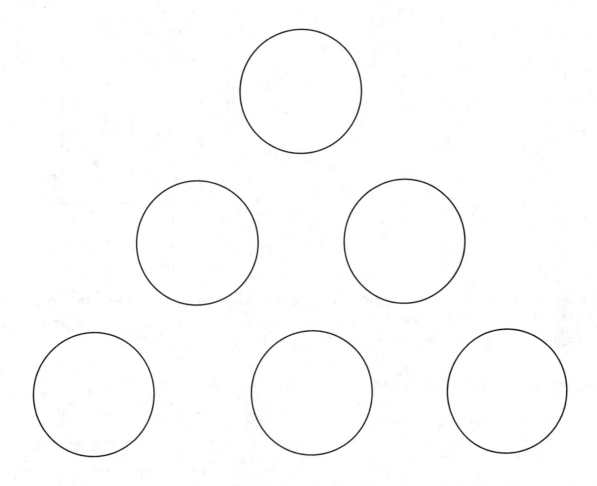

RB-904083 Brain Benders

BREAK THE CUBE

A large cube measures 2 cubes x 2 cubes x 2 cubes. Each side of the large cube is painted a different color. The sides of the small cubes that touch other small cubes are not painted. The colors are red, orange, yellow, green, blue, and purple.

If broken apart, how many cubes will have:

0 colors? _____

1 color? _____

2 colors? _____

3 colors? _____

4 colors? _____

5 colors? _____

6 colors? _____

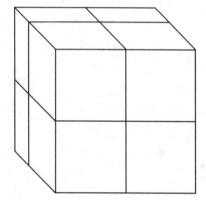

A large cube measures 3 cubes x 3 cubes x 3 cubes. Each side of the large cube is painted a different color. The sides of the small cubes that touch other small cubes are not painted. The colors are red, orange, yellow, green, blue, and purple.

If broken apart, how many cubes will have:

0 colors? _____

1 color? _____

2 colors? _____

3 colors? _____

4 colors? _____

5 colors? _____

6 colors? _____

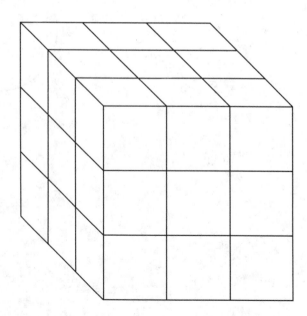

TOOTHPICK TRIANGLES

Jonathan uses 3 toothpicks to make a triangle.

Jonathan makes 3 triangles in the second row. He uses 6 more toothpicks.

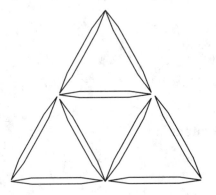

1. How many triangles will be in the 6th row? _____

2. How many toothpicks will Jonathan use in all? _____

3. Jonathan decides to make a 7th row. If he follows the same pattern, how many triangles will there be in all? _____

RB-904083 Brain Benders

X IS TO Y

Circle the letter in front of the answer that correctly completes each analogy.

1. Supermarket is to groceries as restaurant is to
   A. meals.   B. waiter.   C. chefs.   D. plates.

2. Car is to garage as hamburger is to
   A. food.   B. ketchup.   C. cow.   D. bun.

3. Scissors are to cutting as crayons are to
   A. colorful.   B. art.   C. coloring.   D. wax.

4. Doctor is to heal as microwave is to
   A. cool.   B. appliance.   C. kitchen.   D. heat.

5. Artist is to illustration as architect is to
   A. building.   B. blueprint.   C. steel.   D. city.

6. Dark is to bright as wet is to
   A. moist.   B. dry.   C. hard.   D. moldy.

7. Stove is to burner as taco is to
   A. food.   B. nachos.   C. warm.   D. tortilla.

8. Pleasure is to smile as pain is to
   A. grimace.   B. suffer.   C. aspirin.   D. sad.

9. Cat is to milk as garden is to
   A. plants.   B. farmer.   C. rain.   D. growth.

10. School is to fish as flock is to
    A. puppies.   B. cows.   C. turtles.   D. geese.

RB-904083 Brain Benders   © Rainbow Bridge Publishing

Circle the letter in front of the answer that correctly completes each analogy.

1. Chapter is to book as act is to
   A. novel.   B. comedy.   C. play.   D. sitcom.

2. Telescope is to microscope as star is to
   A. planet.   B. glass.   C. cell.   D. universe.

3. Omniscient is to omnipotent as knowledge is to
   A. hope.   B. power.   C. fear.   D. despair.

4. In is to import as out is to
   A. exit.   B. export.   C. exult.   D. expose.

5. Thrifty is to miserly as smart is to
   A. cheap.   B. foolish.   C. gullible.   D. brilliant.

6. Waltz is to dance as oak is to
   A. acorn.   B. tree.   C. pine.   D. tango.

7. Glass is to transparent as wood is to
   A. clear.   B. opaque.   C. pine.   D. fragile.

8. Reveal is to divulge as hide is to
   A. discover.   B. imagine.   C. conceal.   D. inform.

9. Assertive is to passive as definite is to
   A. certain.   B. exact.   C. define.   D. vague.

10. Stiff is to flexible as empty is to
    A. low.   B. rigid.   C. full.   D. elastic.

          RB-904083 Brain Benders

WORD EQUATIONS

The puzzles below are word equations. In each question, the bold letters represent specific words. When combined, the letters and numbers represent a common fact or phrase. Write the phrase on the line. A clue is provided in parentheses after each equation.

1. 365 **D** in a **Y** (Happy Birthday!)

   _____

2. 100 **Y** in a **F F** (Touchdown!)

   _____

3. 54 **C** in a **D** with the **J** (Deal them.)

   _____

4. 50 **S** on the **A F** (Oh, say can you see?)

   _____

5. 8 **L** on a **S** (webs)

   _____

6. 5 **V** in the **E A** (and sometimes Y)

   _____

7. 24 **H** in a **D** (and tomorrow)

   _____

8. 26 **L** of the **E A** (Spell it.)

   _____

9. 7 **D** in a **W** (52 in a year)

   _____

10. 18 **H** on a **G C** (Fore!)

    _____

11. 5 **T** on a **F** (Stand up!)

    _____

12. 3 **W** on a **T** (before a bicycle)

    _____

13. 8 **A** on an **O** (in the ocean)

    _____

14. 9 **L** of a **C** (Meow!)

    _____

WORD EQUATIONS

The puzzles below are word equations. In each question, the bold letters represent specific words. When combined, the letters and numbers represent a common fact or phrase. Write the phrase on the line. A clue is provided in parentheses after each equation.

1. 1492 **C S** the **O B** (I see land!)

   _____

2. 24 **K** in **P G** (jewelry)

   _____

3. 86,400 **S** in a **D** (24 hours)

   _____

4. 1 **W** on a **U** (Balance is important.)

   _____

5. 9 **P** on a **B T** (You're out!)

   _____

6. 112 **E** in the **P T** (You can't eat off of this one!)

   _____

7. 9 **J** on the **U S S C** (Guilty!)

   _____

8. 1,000 **M** in a **K** (a long way to run)

   _____

9. 7 **W** of the **W** (impressive sights)

   _____

10. 3.14 **V** of **P** to the **S D P** (Circle it.)

    _____

11. 36 **B K** on a **P** (Play it again, Sam.)

    _____

12. 90 **D** in a **R A** (not a left)

    _____

13. 3 **B M, S H T R** (They cannot see.)

    _____

14. 23 **P** of **C** in a **H C** (your physical characteristics)

    _____

RB-904083 Brain Benders

Matt, Rick, Amanda, and Trey are new students in school. Each is from a different state: Alaska, Hawaii, New Jersey, and Vermont. Each student owns a different pet: a python, a dog, a goldfish, and a frog. Use the chart and the clues below to determine where each student is from and the type of pet he owns.

1. The student from New Jersey has a mammal for a pet.
2. A boy came from Hawaii and owns the frog.
3. Matt's pet does not have legs.
4. Rick does not own a fish or a frog.
5. All of the boys own either a reptile or a mammal.
6. Amanda lived further north than anyone else.
7. Rick had to travel north to visit Matt.

	Python	Dog	Goldfish	Frog
Matt		New Jersey		
Rick		New Jersey		
Amanda		New Jersey		
Trey		New Jersey		

Jane, Judy, Chuck, and Bill have different jobs: lifeguard, lawyer, pilot, and professor. Each drives a different type of vehicle: truck, motorcycle, bike, or car. Use the chart and the clues below to determine what each person's job is and what type of vehicle she drives.

1. Jane is afraid of flying.
2. Judy gets to her office on a vehicle that has two wheels.
3. For Chuck's job, he is often in two or three states a day.
4. The person who is the lifeguard also drives the truck.
5. A man rides a bicycle to his job.
6. A man needs a large trunk to bring graded papers back and forth to work.

	Lifeguard	Lawyer	Pilot	Professor
Jane			X	
Judy				
Chuck				
Bill				

RB-904083 Brain Benders

Nick, Joey, Beki, and Carmen all ran in the town's annual road race. Each had a different number: 2, 34, 13, and 20. Each person finished in a different amount of time: 10 minutes, 11 minutes 30 seconds, 12 minutes, and 14 minutes. Use the information below and deductive reasoning to determine each person's jersey number and the amount of time it took him to finish the race.

1. The runner with the lowest jersey number also had the slowest time.
2. Nick's jersey number was 18 greater than Carmen's.
3. A man had the fastest finishing time in the race.
4. When you add the digits of Beki's jersey number, you get 7.
5. Nick finished 2 minutes faster than Beki.

	2	34	13	20
Nick				
Joey				
Beki				
Carmen				

Eboni, Julie, Ben, and Dante are athletes. Each participates in a different sport: tennis, golf, skating, and track. One day, they were all sitting at a square table. Use the information below and deductive reasoning to determine each person's sport and to label the drawing with where each athlete is sitting and what sport she plays.

1. The runner sat across from Dante.
2. The tennis player sat on Julie's right.
3. Dante and Julie sat next to each other.
4. A man sat to the left of the runner.
5. The skater sat to the left of the tennis player.

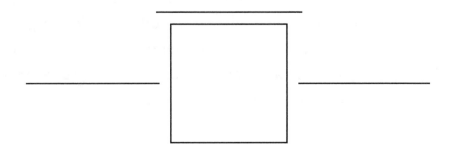

    RB-904083 Brain Benders

ODD WORD OUT

Determine which word or group of words does not belong in each paragraph below. Write each misused word and the word that should replace it on the line below each paragraph.

1. You probably know that Benjamin Franklin is a famous inventor, but did you know that he spent most of his early life as a printer? When he was only 12 years old, he began working as an apprentice in his brother's printing shop. When Franklin moved to Philadelphia, Pennsylvania, in 1928, he opened his own printing shop, where he published his own Web site called the *Pennsylvania Gazette*. He also published *Poor Richard's Almanack* annually, which contained a calendar, weather predictions, poems, and astrological information. It also contained many of Franklin's famous proverbs, such as "Early to bed, early to rise, makes a man healthy, wealthy, and wise."

_____

2. The oceans are an important natural resource for humans. Plants and animals that live in the ocean provide humans with food and medicines. People also use the ocean for recreation. Most importantly, microscopic marine life helps support life on Earth. At least half of the carbon dioxide that we breathe comes from the photosynthesis of marine plants. It is important that we protect the world's oceans.

_____

3. One of the Seven Wonders of the World is the statue of Zeus at Olympia in ancient Greece. In ancient times, people traveled to Olympia to honor and worship Zeus, the king of the gods. The Greek sculptor Phidias of Athens, who was considered the best sculptor in Greece, was chosen to create the statue of Zeus. Phidias made his statue of Zeus sitting on an carved wooden throne decorated with gold, ivory, ebony, and precocious stones. Zeus's feet were resting on a golden footstool. His skin was made of ivory, and his clothing, bear, and hair were made of gold. His eyes were made of gems. The statue of Zeus was a wonder to everyone who saw it.

_____

RB-904083 Brain Benders

OXYMORONS

An oxymoron is a figure of speech that is created when words with opposite or contradictory meanings are used together. For example, the phrase *jumbo shrimp* is an oxymoron, because the word *jumbo* means large and the word *shrimp* can be used to mean small. Underline the oxymoron in each sentence below. Then, on the line provided, explain why the phrase is contradictory.

1. To get her student identification badge, she will need an original copy of her birth certificate.

   _____

2. I want to have an exact estimate of the number of people coming to the party, so please RSVP to the invitation.

   _____

3. The contestants performed in random order.

   _____

4. When the lecturer walked toward the podium, a deafening silence filled the auditorium.

   _____

5. It didn't take long for me to notice that the report I was reading was full of omissions.

   _____

6. The home owner's measurements were almost exact.

   _____

7. I called James to see if he is coming to the party, and he said that he's a definite maybe.

   _____

8. One of the things I like about Kelly is that she is hopelessly optimistic.

   _____

 RB-904083 Brain Benders

OXYMORONS

An oxymoron is a figure of speech that is created when words with opposite or contradictory meanings are used together. For example, the phrase *jumbo shrimp* is an oxymoron, because the word *jumbo* means large and the word *shrimp* can be used to mean small. Underline the oxymoron in each sentence below. Then, on the line provided, explain why the phrase is contradictory.

1. Her explanation of the problem was a slight exaggeration of the situation.

   _____

2. The pilot leveled the plane and set the controls to autopilot.

   _____

3. Billy tried to act naturally when he was caught eating cookies before dinner.

   _____

4. Sally felt like she was alone in the crowd because she was the only girl in the entire class.

   _____

5. Darrell was amazed by the baby grand piano in his friend's house.

   _____

6. Chuck used invisible ink to write the letter to his grandmother.

   _____

7. When Paris spilled the milk on the photograph, it was a minor disaster.

   _____

8. Nicole's mom wanted to cook steak for dinner, but the meat had freezer burn.

   _____

9. During a scary scene in the movie, Fernando got a numb feeling in his feet.

   _____

10. I was very hungry, so my sister gave me the larger half of the pizza.

    _____

RB-904083 Brain Benders

PALINDROMES AND REFLECTIONS

A palindrome is a word, phrase or sentence that means the same thing when read forward and backward. Eye is an example of a palindrome. Think of all of the palindromes that you can. List them on the lines below. HINT: Try to think of words that begin and end with the same letter.

_____   _____   _____

_____   _____   _____

_____   _____   _____

_____   _____   _____

_____   _____   _____

Unlike a palindrome, a reflection forms a new word when it is spelled backward. The word swap is an example of a reflection; spelled backward, it makes the word paws. Fill in each blank below with the reflection that best fits the clue.

1. a storage place for clothes _____

    a sum offered for the detection of a criminal _____

2. another word for students _____

    a mistake or error _____

3. to steal everything from a store _____

    an object for completing work _____

4. an area of a hospital _____

    to create a picture _____

5. to break into two pieces quickly_____

    objects used for cooking food _____

RB-904083 Brain Benders

WORD REFLECTIONS

A reflection is a word that forms a new word when it is spelled backward. Fill in each blank below with the reflection that best fits the clue.

1. a type of cup/candy that is chewed repeatedly _____

2. an untruthful person/path of a train _____

3. item worn by babies/to get money back that is loaned _____

4. way to rest when tired/the coverings of bananas, oranges, and grapefruit _____

5. a circle/a small body of water used to cool off in the summer _____

6. delicious treats after a meal/to be upset and worried _____

7. a forest mammal/a freshwater plant _____

8. the rising and falling of the ocean level/to correct grammar _____

9. to move smoothly/a pack hunting animal _____

10. hollow tube used for drinking/growths on skin caused by a virus _____

11. a thin object that sticks to another surface/a way shoe strings are tied _____

12. a series of many long battles/uncooked _____

RB-904083 Brain Benders

CHANGE-A-WORD

Change the word at the top of each list to the word at the bottom of each list by removing one letter at a time. Each change must make a new word.

1. women

   _____

   _____

   me

2. fused

   _____

   _____

   us

3. spine

   _____

   _____

   in

4. start

   A. _____

   B. _____

   at

5. brush

   _____

   _____

   us

6. splash

   _____

   _____

   _____

   as

7. chirps

   _____

   _____

   _____

   is

8. thinks

   _____

   _____

   _____

   in

LETTER SWAPS

Change the word at the top of the list into the word at the bottom of the list by replacing one letter in the word at a time. Each change must make a new word.

1. fear

    _____

    _____

    _____

    keep

2. dusty

    _____

    _____

    _____

    mines

3. give

    _____

    _____

    _____

    take

4. camp

    _____

    _____

    _____

    fire

5. party

    _____

    _____

    _____

    _____

    dunes

6. timer

    _____

    _____

    _____

    _____

    dunks

RB-904083 Brain Benders

PERPLEXING PUZZLES

The puzzles below use letters, words, and numbers as clues to represent an idea, a popular phrase, or a saying. Often, the placement and size of the words can help convey the puzzle's meaning. Look at the puzzles below. Write the phrase, saying, or idea the clues represent on the line below each puzzle.

1. **Funny**   **Funny**
    Words   **Words**
    Words   **Words**

    _____

2. **All** world

    _____

3. **thodeepught**

    _____

4. **PRO**
    MISE

    _____

5. **head**

    heels

    _____

6. **time time**

    _____

RB-904083 Brain Benders

PERPLEXING PUZZLES

The puzzles below use letters, words, and numbers as clues to represent an idea, a popular phrase, or a saying. Often, the placement and size of the words can help convey the puzzle's meaning. Look at the puzzles below. Write the phrase, saying, or idea the clues represent on the line below each puzzle.

1. cut ◄————————

    cut cut cut
    cut cut cut

    _____

2. little little
    late   late

    _____

3. **174safety659**

    _____

4. **the calm the storm**

    _____

5. **aallll**

    _____

6. H
    G   O
    Z
        ↗
      ⁄ S

    _____

RB-904083 Brain Benders

PERPLEXING PUZZLES

The puzzles below use letters, words, and numbers as clues to represent an idea, a popular phrase, or a saying. Often, the placement and size of the words can help convey the puzzle's meaning. Look at the puzzles below. Write the phrase, saying, or idea the clues represent on the line below each puzzle.

1.
```
E       E
A       A
R       R
T       T
H       H
```

_____

2.
```
M CE
M CE
M CE
```

_____

3.   **PAWALKRK**

_____

4.   **1,000,000 air**

_____

5.   **Chimadena**

_____

6.
1. glance
2.
3. glance
4. glance
5. glance

_____

RB-904083 Brain Benders

FRACTURED WORDS

Seventeen words that are commonly heard in school have been broken into two or three parts and placed into the chart below. Put the words back together on the lines provided. Use each part only once.

du	mar	tory	as	ion
ten	de	time	ti	ap
li	sign	gra	cuse	ence
ex	al	re	at	work
sci	note	ate	ply	dy
geb	at	tude	ra	sten
book	tion	tent	lunch	gram
home	his	tar	cess	ment

1. _____

2. _____

3. _____

4. _____

5. _____

6. _____

7. _____

8. _____

9. _____

10. _____

11. _____

12. _____

13. _____

14. _____

15. _____

16. _____

17. _____

FRACTURED WORDS

Seventeen words that are commonly heard in sports have been broken into two or three parts and placed into the chart below. Put the words back together on the lines provided. Use each part only once.

tice	ner	ble	com	ley
out	tour	der	bask	part
fair	tute	ee	in	time
pire	pen	sti	na	drib
erun	et	ple	for	re
ter	vol	quar	um	tion
way	prac	alty	ward	ment
sub	fiel	hom	fer	back

1. _____

2. _____

3. _____

4. _____

5. _____

6. _____

7. _____

8. _____

9. _____

10. _____

11. _____

12. _____

13. _____

14. _____

15. _____

16. _____

17. _____

RB-904083 Brain Benders

FRACTURED WORDS

Seventeen words commonly associated with eating have been broken into two or three parts and placed into the chart below. Put the words back together on the lines provided. Use each part only once.

cu	va	trée	it	to
por	tas	or	wa	over
cof	choc	cas	fru	late
des	ple	pot	fri	bé
cal	see	fer	piz	en
o	ie	suc	turn	lent
nil	flam	sert	ap	ty
za	a	fee	tion	la

1. _____
2. _____
3. _____
4. _____
5. _____
6. _____
7. _____
8. _____
9. _____
10. _____
11. _____
12. _____
13. _____
14. _____
15. _____
16. _____
17. _____

RB-904083 Brain Benders

Eight words often associated with reading and writing have been broken into pieces. Use the syllables in the chart below to answer each clue. Write the words on the lines. Each syllable is used once.

a	mag	al	ce	pe	re
let	rec	box	pa	tions	zine
rec	al	news	ter	jou	i
rn	mes	sage	di	per	

1. Tells what's going on each day _____

2. Read for fun or information _____

3. A place to write secrets_____

4. Found on a breakfast table _____

5. Placed in a mailbox _____

6. Explains how to do something_____

7. Followed when cooking _____

8. Found in a bottle or beside the phone _____

RB-904083 Brain Benders

WORD ORIGINS

Write the correct word and identify each answer as an eponym, an acronym, or a portmanteau word. Remember: An eponym is a name or a noun that is formed from the name of a person. Acronyms are words that are formed from the initial letters of other words. A portmanteau word blends the sounds and meanings of two words into a single new word.

America	RADAR	motel	sandwich
brunch	LASER	SCUBA	Internet

1. light amplification by stimulation emission of radiation

   _____   _____

2. self-contained underwater breathing apparatus

   _____   _____

3. radio detecting and range

   _____   _____

4. from the name of Amerigo Vespucci, an explorer

   _____   _____

5. motor + hotel

   _____   _____

6. breakfast + lunch

   _____   _____

7. from the title, the fourth Earl of Sandwich

   _____   _____

8. international + network

   _____   _____

RB-904083 Brain Benders

WORD SQUARES

Determine the words that are being defined to the right of each grid. Then, write the four-letter words that can be read across or down.

1.

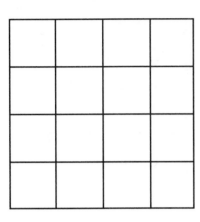

to indicate, demonstrate

a residence, abode

to leave out

moistens

2.

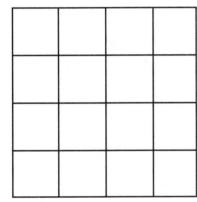

to plead, advocate strongly

a space in a building

a desert plateau in East Asia

to send out, give forth

3.

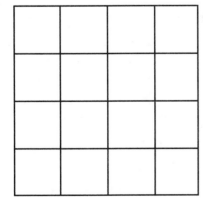

slang for photographs

a thought or scheme

a penny, one-hundredth of a dollar

to satisfy with more than enough

RB-904083 Brain Benders

ROOT WORDS

Circle the letter in front of the correct meaning for each root. Then, on the lines provided, write two words that contain the root.

1. therm   A. above   B. heat   C. after

_____ _____

2. anti   A. against   B. for   C. book

_____ _____

3. morph   A. love   B. form   C. change

_____ _____

4. biblio   A. form   B. good   C. book

_____ _____

5. cardio   A. heart   B. measure   C. power

_____ _____

6. bio   A. sea   B. far   C. life

_____ _____

7. tri   A. one   B. two   C. three

_____ _____

8. ology   A. study of   B. fear   C. all

_____ _____

9. chron   A. time   B. fear   C. study of

_____ _____

10. port   A. carry   B. out   C. in

_____ _____

RB-904083 Brain Benders

idioms

Use the clues to unscramble each idiom. Write each idiom on the line.

1. There can be many ways of doing something.

   lead roads Rome all to

   _____

2. forced to decide between unpleasant choices

   and between hard rock a place a

   _____

3. unable to think of a word that you know

   of the tongue on tip your

   _____

4. to hear something and then immediately forget it

   the in out ear one other and

   _____

5. to accept more responsibility than you can handle

   chew more bite than can you off

   _____

6. If you want to be successful, don't procrastinate.

   catches bird worm the early the

   _____

7. If something is free, don't be too critical of it.

   in look horse the don't a gift mouth

   _____

FANTASTIC PHRASES

Rearrange the letters in the first word to create a second word that completes a two-word phrase. For example, the letters in *best* can be rearranged to spell *bets* to complete the phrase *best bets.* A clue is provided in parentheses after each word.

1. outer (Way to go!) _____

2. direct (given when it's due) _____

3. actors (equal parts) _____

4. ocean (Don't tip it over!) _____

5. demo (That's the way!) _____

6. lovely (a tennis shot) _____

7. remote (in the night sky) _____

8. ruthless (Hurry up!) _____

9. versatile (kin) _____

10. nameless (people who go go door to door) _____

RB-904083 Brain Benders

WORD BUDDIES

Start with the first pair of words. Make the next word pair using the last word from the previous word pair as the first word. Words that are made must be either compound words or "word buddies" (two words that are often used together). The goal is to reach the last word or pair of words.

ball	dragon	dragon	finger	finger	fly	fly	ring	snap	snap

1. key ring
2. _____
3. _____
4. _____
5. _____
6. _____
7. ball game

bath	bath	bird	bird	blue	line	out	out	time	time

8. sky blue
9. _____
10. _____
11. _____
12. _____
13. _____
14. lineup

RB-904083 Brain Benders

WORD BUDDIES

Start with the first word or pair of words. Make the next word pair using the last word from the previous word pair as the first word. Words that are made must be either compound words or "word buddies" (two words that are often used together). The goal is to reach the last word.

box	box	lunch	lunch	mail	out	out	side	time	time

1. airmail
2. _____
3. _____
4. _____
5. _____
6. _____
7. sidewalk

back	back	door	door	hand	horse	horse	saw	saw	step

8. left hand
9. _____
10. _____
11. _____
12. _____
13. _____
14. stepladder

RB-904083 Brain Benders

TWiSTED WORDS

Find the seven-letter word hidden in each grid. The letters in the word must touch.
Words can be found horizontally, vertically, backward, and forward, but not diagonally.
HINT: Circle the letters that go together.

1.

M	E	R	U
H	I	C	T
K	P	O	Y
S	D	L	N

The word is _____.

2.

T	C	A	D
L	E	J	Y
I	W	O	R
N	U	S	P

The word is _____.

3.

Y	C	O	T
R	E	X	U
F	H	P	L
S	N	I	A

The word is _____.

4.

R	Q	U	Y
E	A	Z	C
P	D	I	N
S	H	O	G

The word is _____.

RB-904083 Brain Benders

Find the seven-letter word hidden in each grid. The letters in the word must touch. Words can be found horizontally, vertically, backward, and forward, but not diagonally. HINT: Circle the letters that go together.

1.

U	Y	S	E
R	A	G	O
P	M	R	I
H	M	A	V

The word is _____.

2.

P	S	I	T
K	A	P	A
Z	C	N	L
B	U	Y	O

The word is _____.

3.

R	O	Z	K
B	S	K	M
C	T	L	U
I	P	E	D

The word is _____.

4.

Y	L	O	P
E	W	S	G
A	R	I	N
M	U	T	I

The word is _____.

RB-904083 Brain Benders

P. 3—Numbers in a Line
1. 40, 41, 42; **2.** 39, 41, 43; **3.** 151, 152, 153; **4.** 150, 152, 154; **5.** 262, 263, 264; **6.** 48, 50, 52; **7.** 57, 59, 61, 63; **8.** 18, 19, 20, 21, 22; **9.** 28, 29, 30, 31, 32; **10.** 98, 99, 100, 101, 102

P. 4—Missing Signs
1. 48 + 12 = 60; **2.** 55 x 5 = 275; **3.** 10 x 10 = 100; **4.** 210 ÷ 10 = 21; **5.** 117 – 10 = 107; **6.** 635 – 7 = 628; **7.** 303 + 30 = 333; **8.** 35 x 60 = 2,100; **9.** 948 ÷ 2 = 474; **10.** 87 x 52 = 4,524

P. 5—Backward Numbers
The sums in both sets of problems match: 88, 132, 143, 99, 121, 110. Only two-digit problems in which the sum of the ones digits equals the sum of the tens digits will give the same sum when written backward.

P. 6—Number Switch
1. 26 + 8 = 34　　**2.** 79 + 6 = 85
3. 41 – 5 = 36　　**4.** 73 – 8 = 65
5. 12 x 8 = 96　　**6.** 24 x 3 = 72
7. 34 + 61 = 95　**8.** 28 + 17 = 45

P. 7—Calculator Riddles
1. 338, bee; **2.** 14, hi; **3.** 35,006, goose; **4.** 53,704, holes; **5.** 5,637, legs; **6.** 53,045, shoes; **7.** 304,304, hoe, hoe

P. 8—At the Bakery
1. Mrs. Lee, 24; Mr. Lang, 36; Ms. Lopez, 12; Mrs. Brenner, 12 Mr. Murray, 4; Ryan, 4; **2.** 96

P. 9—A Family Portrait
1. There are 24 possible arrangements. **2.** Multiply the number of elements: 4 x 3 x 2 x 1 = 24. To find out how many different arrangements there are with 5 people, you can multiply 5 x 4 x 3 x 2 x 1 to get 120.

P. 10—Amazing Sums
110 + 999 = 1,109
1,109 + 9,999 = 11,108
11,108 + 99,999 = 111,107
111,107 + 999,999 = 1,111,106
1,111,106 + 9,999,999 = 11,111,105
11,111,105 + 99,999,999 = 111,111,104
111,111,104 + 999,999,999 = 1,111,111,103
Patterns: The number of times that 1 appears in the answer increases with each new sum. The ones digit decreases by 1 each time. The number of digits in one addend equals the number of digits in the other addend each time.

P. 11—Mysterious Multiplication
1. 413,413; **2.** 736,736; **3.** 80,080; **4.** 653,653; **5.** 999,999 Each time a three-digit number is multiplied by 11 and 91, or 1,001. If XYZ stands for a three-digit number, then multiplying produces 1,001 groups of XYZ altogether—1,000 groups of XYZ and 1 group of XYZ. This results in the number XYZ,000 + XYZ—or XYZ,XYZ.

P. 12—Crisscross
1. The missing number in the third figure is 2. **Pattern:** Take the sum of the top and bottom numbers and divide it by the sum of the left and right numbers; write the answer in the center circle; **2.** The missing number in the third figure is 3. **Pattern:** Take the product of the top and bottom numbers and divide it by the product of the left and right numbers; write the answer in the center circle; **3. Pattern:** Take the product of the top and bottom numbers and divide it by the sum of the left and right numbers. The missing number in the third figure is 3.

P. 13—Dotted Hexagons

1. 18 dots were used (4 dots per side); **2.** 18, 24, 30; **3.** Subtract 1 from the number of dots used per side. Then, multiply the result by 6. For a hexagon with 20 dots per side, there would be (20 – 1) x 6 dots, or 114.

P. 14—Paper Patterns
1. 31; **2.** The formula is 3(n – 1) + 1, in which n stands for the number of the figure. Take the number of the figure and subtract 1. Then, multiply by 3 and add 1. For example, to find the number of squares needed for the 10th figure, subtract 1 from 10 to get 9. Then, multiply by 3 to get 27. Add 1 to get 28, the number of squares needed; **3.** 19; **4.** The formula is 2(n – 1) + 1. Take the number of the figure and subtract 1. Then, multiply by 2 and add 1. For example, to find the number of squares needed for the 10th figure, subtract 1 from 10 to get 9. Then, multiply by 2 to get 18. Finally, add 1 to get 19, the number of squares needed.

P. 15—Dots and Squares
For the 3 x 3 grid, there are 6 possible squares. For the 4 x 4 grid, there are 22 possible squares.

P. 16—Circle Puzzles
First circle　　Second circle

RB-904083 Brain Benders

P. 17—Shapes and Numbers

◯ = 3

△ = 2

▢ = 4

◇ = 5

⬡ = 1

The missing sums are 16, 10, and 12.

P. 18—Number Cubes

Answers will vary. Possible solutions for the first set of given numbers may include:

2	9	4	15
7	5	3	15
6	1	8	15
15	15	15	

8	1	6	15
3	5	7	15
4	9	2	15
15	15	15	

4	3	8	15
9	5	1	15
2	7	6	15
15	15	15	

Set 2: Answers will vary. The patterns will work for multiples of 2, 3, and 4.

P. 19—Number Riddles

1. 36   **2.** 9   **3.** 8
4. 50   **5.** 5   **6.** 1
7. 26   **8.** 10   **9.** 124

P. 20—Find the Numbers

Set A: M = 6   R = 3   T = 2
Set B: B = 9   J = 8   S = 1
Set C: G = 8   K = 4   Z = 6
Set D: C = 1   G = 5   U = 3

P. 21—Hidden Numbers

Answers will vary. The following are examples of correct answers:

1. (8 ÷ 2 + 2) ÷ 2 = 3
  2 x 9 ÷ 6 = 3
  6 ÷ 2 = 3
  9 ÷ (2 + 1) = 3
  8 − 2 − 1 − 2 = 3
  (9 − 5) ÷ 2 + 1 = 3
  7 + 2 − 6 = 3
  4 ÷ 2 + 1 = 3
  10 − 4 ÷ 2 = 3
2. 2 + 4 − 1 = 5
  2 x 4 − 3 = 5
  7 − 2 = 5
  10 x 1 − (2 + 3) = 5
  11 − 8 + 2 = 5
3. 6 x 2 − 2 = 10
  2 x 3 + 4 = 10
  6 + 2 + 2 = 10
  4 x 3 − 2 = 10
  (9 x 4) − (5 x 7) + 6 + 2 + 2 − 1 = 10

P. 22—Missing Steps

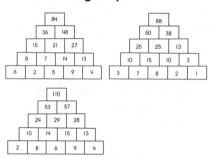

P. 23—Missing Steps

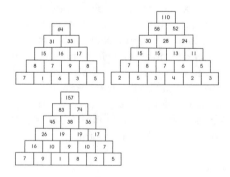

P. 24—Puzzle It Out

Set A: Missing number—6; Answers will vary. **Rule:** If *a* = number in top row, *b* and *c* = numbers in second row, and *d* and *e* = numbers in third row—then *b* − *c* = *f*, *d* − *e* = *g*, and *f* x *g* = *a*

Set B: Missing number—1; Answers will vary. **Rule:** If *a* = number in top row, *b* and *c* = numbers in second row, and *d* and *e* = numbers in third row—then *b* x *c* = *f*, *d* x *e* = *g*, and *f* − *g* = *a*

Set C: Missing number—72; Answers will vary. **Rule:** If *a* = number in top row, *b* and *c* = numbers in second row, and *d* and *e* = numbers in third row—then *b* + *d* = *f*, *c* + *e* = *g*, and *f* x *g* = *a*

P. 25—Hide-and-Seek

P. 26—The Total

Badgers, 24
Bobcats, 9
Hornets, 12
Wolfpack, 20
Tornadoes, 7

1. 6 points
2. 10 points
3. 14 points

P. 27—Mystery Squares

33	38	39	110
41	32	37	110
36	40	34	110
110	110	110	

113	118	119	350
121	112	117	350
116	120	114	350
350	350	350	

P. 28—Mystery Squares
1.

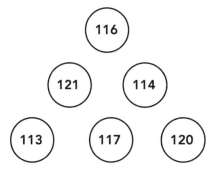

2. Answers will vary.

P. 29—Mystery Triangle

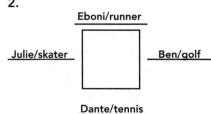

P. 30—Break the Cube
1. All of the cubes will have 3 colors. 2. One cube will have 0 colors. Four cubes will have 1 color. Eight cubes will have 2 colors. Eight cubes will have 3 colors.

P. 31—Toothpick Triangles
1. 18 triangles are in the 6th row.
2. Nathan will use 63 toothpicks in all.
3. There will be 49 triangles in all.

P. 32—X Is to Y
1. A; 2. D; 3. C; 4. D; 5. B; 6. B;
7. D; 8. A; 9. C; 10. D

P. 33—X Is to Y
1. C; 2. C; 3. B; 4. B; 5. D; 6. B;
7. B; 8. C; 9. D; 10. C

P. 34—Word Equations
1. 365 days in a year; 2. 100 yards in a football field; 3. 54 cards in a deck with the jokers; 4. 50 stars on the American flag; 5. 8 legs on a spider; 6. 5 vowels in the English alphabet; 7. 24 hours in a day;
8. 26 letters in the English alphabet;
9. 7 days in a week; 10. 18 holes

P. 34—continued
on a golf course; 11. 5 toes on a foot; 12. 3 wheels on a tricycle;
13. 8 arms on an octopus;
14. 9 lives of a cat

P. 35—Word Equations
1. 1492 Columbus sailed the ocean blue; 2. 24 karats in pure gold;
3. 86,400 seconds in a day;
4. 1 wheel on a unicycle;
5. 9 players on a baseball team;
6. 112 elements in the periodic table; 7. 9 judges on the United States Supreme Court;
8. 1,000 meters in a kilometer;
9. 7 wonders of the world; 10. 3.14 value of pi to the second decimal place; 11. 36 black keys on a piano;
12. 90 degrees in a right angle;
13. 3 blind mice, see how they run;
14. 23 pairs of chromosomes in a human cell

P. 36—A Good Reason
1. **Matt:** python/Vermont, **Rick:** dog/New Jersey, **Amanda:** goldfish/ Alaska, **Trey:** frog/Hawaii, 2. **Jane:** lifeguard/truck, **Judy:** lawyer/ motorcycle; **Chuck:** pilot, bicycle; **Bill:** professor, car

P. 37—A Good Reason
1. **Nick:** #20/10 minutes
   Joey: #13/11 minutes 30 seconds
   Beki: #34/12 minutes
   Carmen: #2/14 minutes
2.

Eboni/runner

Julie/skater | | Ben/golf

Dante/tennis

P. 38—Odd Word Out
1. ~~Web site~~, *newspaper*
2. ~~carbon dioxide~~, *oxygen*
3. ~~precocious~~, *precious*

P. 39—Oxymorons
Answers will vary. Accept any reasonable explanation. 1. original copy; 2. exact estimate;
3. random order; 4. deafening silence; 5. full of omissions;
6. almost exact; 7. definite maybe
8. hopelessly optimistic

P. 40—Oxymorons
Answers will vary. Accept any reasonable explanation. 1. slight exaggeration; 2. autopilot; 3. act naturally; 4. alone in the crowd;
5. grand piano; 6. invisible ink;
7. minor disaster; 8. freezer burn;
9. numb feeling; 10. larger half;

P. 41—Palindromes and Reflections
Palindromes will vary. 1. drawer, reward; 2. pupils, slipup; 3. loot, tool; 4. ward, draw; 5. snap, pans

P. 42— Word Reflections
1. mug, gum; 2. liar, rail; 3. diaper, repaid; 4. sleep, peels; 5. loop, pool; 6. desserts, stressed; 7. deer, reed; 8. tide, edit; 9. flow, wolf;
10. straw, warts; 11. decal, laced;
12. war, raw

P. 43—Change-a-Word
1. omen, men; 2. used, use; 3. pine, pin; 4. tart, art; 5. bush, bus;
6. slash, lash, ash; 7. chips, hips, his; 8. think, thin, tin

Page 44—Letter Swaps
1. fear, dear, deer, deep, keep;
2. dusty, musty, minty, mints, mines;
3. give, live, like, lake, take;
4. camp, came, fame, fare, fire;
5. party, parts, darts, dares, Danes, dunes; 6. timer, times, dimes, dines, dunes, dunks.

P. 45—Perplexing Puzzles
1. too funny for words; 2. it's small world after all; 3. deep in thought;
4. broken promise; 5. head over heels; 6. time after time

P. 46—Perplexing Puzzles
1. a cut above the rest; 2. too little, too late; 3. safety in numbers;
4. the calm before the storm; 5. all in all; 6. horsing around

P. 47—Perplexing Puzzles
1. down to earth; 2. three blind mice; 3. a walk in the park; 4. made in China; 5. millionaire; 6. neon light

P. 48—Fractured Words
algebra, apply, assignment, attention, attitude, detention, excuse, grammar, graduate, history, homework, listen, notebook, posture, recess, science, tardy

P. 49—Fractured Words
basket, dribble, completion, fairway, forward, home run, infielder, partner, penalty, practice, quarterback, referee, volley, substitute, timeout, tournament, umpire

P. 50—Fractured Words
apple, calorie, chocolate, coffee, dessert, fruit, entree, flambe, fricassee, pizza, portion, potato, succulent, tasty, turnover, vanilla, wafer

P. 51—Breakdown
1. newspaper; 2. magazine;
3. journal; 4. cereal box; 5. letter;
6. directions; 7. recipe; 8. message

P. 52—Word Origins
1. LASER, acronym; 2. SCUBA, acronym; 3. RADAR, acronym;
4. America, eponym; 5. motel, portmanteau word; 6. brunch, portmanteau word; 7. sandwich, eponym; 8. Internet, portmanteau word

P. 53—Word Squares
1. show, home, omit, wets; 2. urge, room, Gobi, emit; 3. pics, idea, cent, sate

P. 54—Root Words
Words will vary.
1. B; 2. A; 3. C; 4. C; 5. A; 6. C;
7. C; 8. A; 9. A; 10. A

P. 55—Idioms
1. All roads lead to Rome.;
2. between a rock and a hard place;
3. on the tip of your tongue; 4. in one ear and out the other; 5. bite off more than you can chew; 6. The early bird catches the worm;
7. Don't look a gift horse in the mouth.

P. 56—Fantastic Phrases
1. route; 2. credit; 3. costar;
4. canoe; 5. mode; 6. volley;
7. meteor; 8. hustlers; 9. relatives;
10. salesmen

P. 57—Word Buddies
1. key ring; 2. ring finger; 3. finger snap; 4. snapdragon; 5. dragon fly;
6. fly ball; 7. ball game; 8. sky blue;
9. blue bird; 10. bird bath; 11. bath time; 12. time out; 13. out line;
14. lineup

P. 58—Word Buddies
1. airmail; 2. mailbox; 3. box lunch;
4. lunchtime; 5. time-out; 6. outside;
7. sidewalk; 8. left hand; 9. hand saw; 10. sawhorse; 11. horseback;
12. back door; 13. doorstep;
14. step ladder

P. 59—Twisted Words
1. picture; 2. project; 3. explain;
4. reading

P. 60—Twisted Words
1. grammar; 2. capital; 3. depicts;
4. writing